Escalators

Kelli Hicks

Scan for Related Titles
and Teacher Resources

Rourke
Educational Media

rourkeeducationalmedia.com

Teaching Focus:

Text features: Labels and Captions- How do the labels and captions help you as you read this book?

Before Reading:

Building Academic Vocabulary and Background Knowledge

Before reading a book, it is important to set the stage for your child or student by using pre-reading strategies. This will help them develop their vocabulary, increase their reading comprehension, and make connections across the curriculum.

1. *Read the title and look at the cover. Let's make predictions about what this book will be about.*
2. *Take a picture walk by talking about the pictures/photographs in the book. Implant the vocabulary as you take the picture walk. Be sure to talk about the text features such as headings, the Table of Contents, glossary, bolded words, captions, charts/diagrams, or index.*
3. *Have students read the first page of text with you then have students read the remaining text.*
4. *Strategy Talk – use to assist students while reading.*
   - *Get your mouth ready*
   - *Look at the picture*
   - *Think...does it make sense*
   - *Think...does it look right*
   - *Think...does it sound right*
   - *Chunk it – by looking for a part you know*
5. *Read it again.*
6. *After reading the book complete the activities below.*

Content Area Vocabulary
Use glossary words in a sentence.

complex
conveyor belt
gears
handrails
houses
truss

After Reading:

Comprehension and Extension Activity

After reading the book, work on the following questions with your child or students in order to check their level of reading comprehension and content mastery.

1. *What are gears? (Summarize)*
2. *Why does the handrail move with the escalator? (Infer)*
3. *How are a conveyor belt and escalator similar? (Asking questions)*
4. *When is a time you used an escalator? Why? (Text to self connection)*

Extension Activity

Think about how escalators help move people. Now compare and contrast escalators, stairs, and elevators. How do they move people? Can they move large objects? Do they need power? Create a triple Venn diagram to help you organize your thoughts.

Table of Contents

Going Up?

You are on the first floor and need to go up. What should you do? You might climb the stairs taking one step at a time.

Maybe you will wait for the elevator doors to open, go in, and press the button for the second floor. Me? I like to ride the escalator!

A Magic Stairway

What is an escalator? It is a moving staircase with steps that go up or down.

Jesse Reno designed the first moving escalator. Built in 1892, it was a ride at an amusement park.

Conveying a Good Idea

The idea for an escalator came from the same design as a **conveyor belt**. A conveyor belt moves items a short distance on a flat surface. You can see a conveyor belt at work in the grocery store.

An escalator is a **complex** conveyor system.

The base is called a **truss**. It is hidden under the stairs and provides support. It also **houses** the escalator's motor.

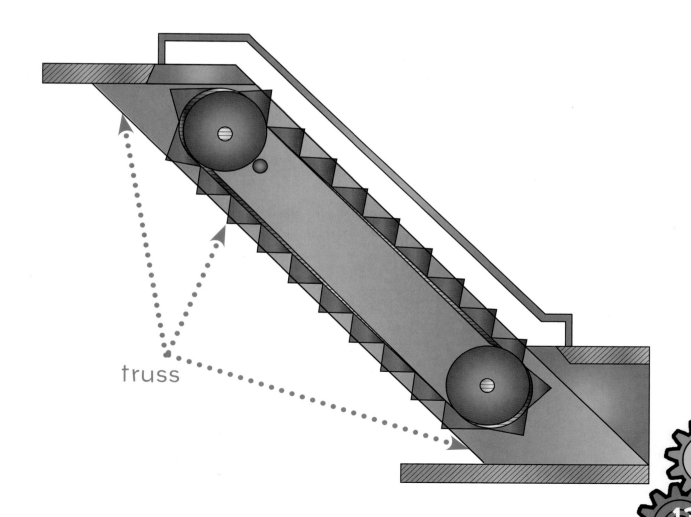

truss

An escalator has two pairs of **gears**. One set is at the top, and the other is at the bottom. The gears have chains that loop around them.

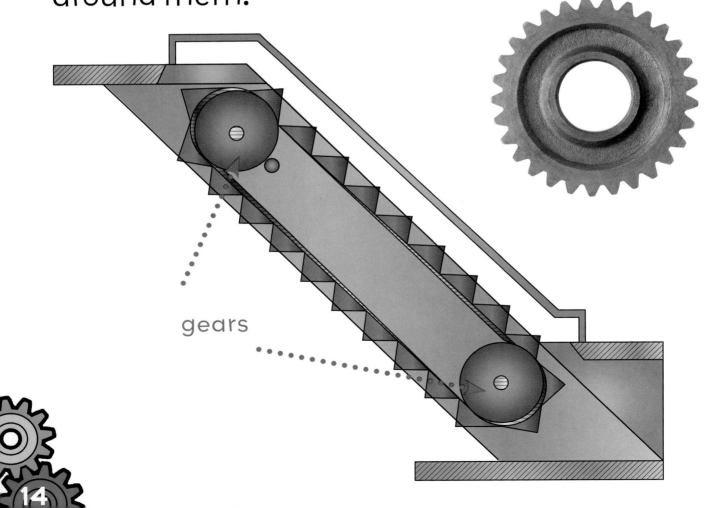

gears

14

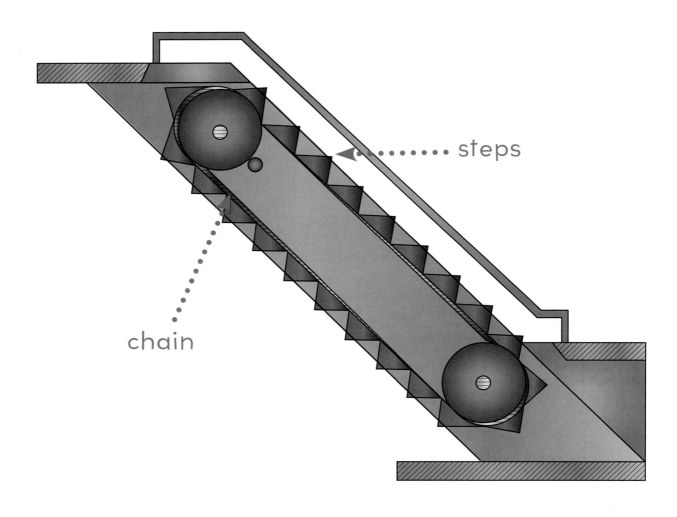

steps

chain

The chains are connected to the steps. As the chains move, the steps move as well.

The steps at the top and the bottom of the escalator flatten to create an even surface. That makes it easier to get on or off the steps.

People riding an escalator hold on to **handrails.** The handrails move at the same speed as the stairs. Covered in rubber, the handrails are also an example of a conveyor belt.

Be safe when riding on an escalator. Always face forward and hold onto the handrail.

Photo Glossary

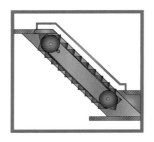

complex (KAHM-pleks): Something that is complicated. Complex machines have many moving parts.

conveyor belt (kuhn-VAY-or belt): This is a continuous band of rubber that moves items from one place to another.

gears (geerz): Gears are a set of wheels with teeth that fit together and move in a machine.

handrails (HAND-raylz): These are narrow, thin rails.

houses (HOUZ-ez): Someplace with a specific purpose or where something is stored.

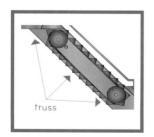

truss

truss (truhs): A truss is a strong frame of beams or bars.

Index

Websites to Visit

www.kids.discovery.com/home/how-does-an-escalator-work

www.engrailhistory.info/r140.html

www.theelevatormuseum.org/esc.php

About the Author

Kelli Hicks is a teacher and author who lives in Tampa, Florida with her family. She can often be found at her computer, running around on the soccer field, or riding the escalator at the shopping mall.

Meet The Author!
www.meetREMauthors.com

www.rourkeeducationalmedia.com

PHOTO CREDITS: Cover © ZargonDesign; title page, 15 © haveseen; page 4 © princessdlaf; page 5 © Nikada; page 7 © ArtMarie; page 8, 23 © Pere Sanz; page 11, 22 © Empire 331; page 12 © Laosi; page 13, 14, 16, 22 © Jen Thomas; page 14, 22 © koosen; page 17 © Joy Fera; page 19 © robeo; page 21, 23 © Forster Forest; page 23 © Luckie8

Edited by: Jill Sherman

Cover design by: Renee Brady
Interior design by: Jen Thomas

Library of Congress PCN Data

Escalators/ Kelli Hicks
(How It Works)
ISBN (hard cover)(alk. paper) 978-1-62717-647-7
ISBN (soft cover) 978-1-62717-769-6
ISBN (e-Book) 978-1-62717-889-1
Library of Congress Control Number: 2014934239
Printed in the United States of America, North Mankato, Minnesota

Also Available as:

ROURKE'S
e-Books